Old Almondbank, Methven and C'

by

P.J.G. Ransom

CW00502220

The Almondbank motor bus looks brand new, the crew have smart new uniforms, and the passengers look posed (as does the girl posting a letter), so this photograph was probably taken to mark the bus's entry into service. The vehicle was almost certainly built on an Italian Lancia chassis and the date is probably 1912 – 'ES' registration numbers appear to have reached the 800s around then. The newspaper placard trumpeting 'Submarine Disaster' is sadly less help in dating the picture than might be expected: such events were all too common, and there were two in that year. The location is outside the former post office in Almondbank Main Street and there is still a bus stop at the same place. Stagecoach buses stop at it today, but are unlikely to be found facing the wrong way on to the traffic!

Text © P.J.G. Ransom, 2010.
First published in the United Kingdom, 2010,
by Stenlake Publishing Ltd.
Telephone: 01290 551122
www.stenlake.co.uk

ISBN 9781840335040

The publishers regret that they cannot supply copies of any pictures featured in this book.

Above: Built in the nineteenth-century, Logiealmond Inn stands on the Harrietfield–Luncarty road. A porch has been added at the front since this photograph was taken, and it is now called The Inn at Chapelhill.

Further Reading

The books listed below were used by the author during his research. None of them is available from Stenlake Publishing. Those interested in finding out more are advised to contact their local bookshop or reference library.

David Marshall Forrester, *Logiealmond*, Oliver and Boyd, 1944.
John Gifford, *Perth and Kinross* (Buildings of Scotland series), Yale University Press, 2007.
Nick Haynes, *Perth & Kinross: an Illustrated Architectural Guide*, Rutland Press, 2000.
Thomas Huxley, *The Almond Valley Past and Present*, Author, 2007.
John Mackay, *The Bleachfields of Perth*, Author, 2008.
W. Robertson Nicoll, *'Ian Maclaren' Life of the Rev. John Watson D.D.*, Hodder & Stoughton, 1908.
James F. Stephens, *Feasibility Study of Methven Castle for Perth & Kinross District Council*, 1979.

Acknowledgements

I must first thank Thomas Huxley, whose publications on the local history of Almondbank and Pitcairngreen are essential for anyone studying the district, for his willingness to share his encyclopaedic knowledge. I have also been much helped by Elaine Mundill and David Willington of Glenalmond College, Allan Proctor of Tulchan House and Clare Lindsay of the Shetland Pony Stud-Book Society. Bob Flockhart and Mike Wilson have kindly helped to identify motor vehicles and a steam locomotive respectively. Marie Geddes pointed me in the right direction to find Bessie Bell and Mary Gray's grave. Staff and regulars in the bar of the Drumtochty Tavern, Harrietfield, responded most helpfully to a stranger who appeared in their midst gabbling about old photographs. I am also indebted for their assistance to Ann Robertson and to the staffs of the A.K. Bell Library, Perth, and the Royal Commission on the Ancient and Historical Monuments of Scotland. My wife Elisabeth and agent Duncan McAra have been as helpful as ever. I am grateful to them all.

Introduction

The district portrayed in these pictures, which date for the most part from the first three decades of the twentieth century, lies near the geographical centre of Scotland – that is to say west and northwest of Perth, and immediately south of the Highland Line. It is not untypical: it contains one small town (Methven), several villages, rural houses big and small, and a large amount of agricultural land of various degrees of fertility. Nor is its history untypical. During the century and a half prior to our period, there had been great improvements in agriculture, communications, living conditions and manufacturing. Nevertheless at the beginning of the twentieth century there were still extremes of wealth and poverty, and of social divisions. But the country as a whole was prosperous and, from the look of these pictures, something of this rubbed off on everyone.

Two features associated with the district did stand out. These were an industry, and an author – both at one time familiar, indeed famous, but now largely forgotten. The industry was textile finishing. This was dependent upon the district's most important natural feature, the swift-flowing River Almond (the Perthshire Almond, that is, for there is another not far away in West Lothian). Somewhat secretive, the river winds its way along the foot of steep slopes which in places transform themselves into high bluffs or sharp and eroded cliffs. Roads seldom follow it closely, and there are few bridges. Less use is being made of the Almond now than at any time in history, but formerly there were innumerable weirs and mills on its course from the Sma' Glen to the Tay. As early as the mediaeval period some of its water was diverted below Almondbank into Perth town lade, also called the King's lade, to power mills on the way to, and within, Perth itself. On the Almond there were, at various times and places, corn mills, lint mills, sawmills, paper mills, cotton-spinning mills, flour mills, barley mills and hydro-electric generating stations. But what was really important was textile finishing.

Initially, this meant bleachfields for linen. Linen, when made, was brown: it needed to be bleached. This was done by boiling it in water made alkaline by wood ash, and spreading it out on the grass for the action of sun, rain and dew to take effect. In the eighteenth century government subsidies encouraged large public bleachfields. Locations where there was a copious supply of pure water were ideal: bleachfields fed by the Almond, or Perth town lade, were eventually established at Ruthvenfield, Huntingtowerfield, Pitcairnfield and Cromwellpark, all these being in the vicinity of Almondbank. There were others nearby. By the end of the eighteenth century, these were the most important bleachfields in Scotland.

But the bleaching process took months. Early in the nineteenth century chemical bleaching was developed and the time was reduced to days. Bleaching now moved wholly under cover, although the bleachworks continued to be referred to as 'bleachfields'. Handling the cloth was mechanised, with machinery powered at first by water, later by steam. Ancillary processes were added such as beetling, dyeing and printing. Cotton was also treated. Changes came gradually, but were largely complete by the early 1900s, with the industry at its height. Subsequently the story was one of gradual decline, but the industry died hard: Huntingtowerfield and Pitcairnfield, the last two bleachworks related to the Almond, closed only in 1982, and Luncarty, last survivor in the district, as recently as 1996. Few traces remain.

Turning to the author, this was Ian Maclaren – or, to give him his real name, the Rev. John Watson, D.D. Watson was a complex character, a minister of the Free Church yet with the Catholic faith in his recent ancestry. Much of his childhood was spent in and around Perth, and subsequently he became, for a few years in the 1870s, Free Church minister of Logiealmond, after which he moved away to Glasgow and later to Liverpool. Logiealmond is the northeastern part of our district, an isolated area where the inhabitants were noted for character and canniness. Watson had evidently absorbed it all, place and people, for when in the 1890s he was persuaded to write some lay material for a magazine to which he was contributing articles on religion, it was to Logiealmond and Perth that he turned for inspiration and setting.

He also turned to his mother's maiden name, preceded by the Gaelic form of his own Christian name, for a *nom-de-plume*. The resultant tales of Scottish country life by Ian Maclaren were well written, penetrating and perceptive: they were an overnight runaway success on both sides of the Atlantic. Maclaren applied fictional names to real places – Logiealmond became 'Drumtochty' for instance – and these became better and more widely known than the real names. Postcards were published with the fictional place name in the caption, sometimes without comment. Some of these are reproduced on the pages which follow. Yet Maclaren's writings were also highly sentimental and used for their dialogue a phonetic rendering of the speech of the district. Such things perhaps no longer appeal to today's tastes, and help to explain why the author and his work are so little known today.

The whole area covered by this book appears on Ordnance Survey 1:50,000 map sheet 52. Readers may find it helpful to have a copy handy.

Huntingtowerfield works dated from the establishment of a bleachfield in 1775. Water was supplied from Perth town lade. By about 1912, the date of this picture, the linen industry was at its most prosperous and the works belonged to Lumsden & Mackenzie, a noted local firm. Steam power was being used as well as water power, and electricity was being generated to operate the machinery used in the chemical bleaching and finishing processes. After eventual closure in 1982 the works was demolished and its site is now occupied by houses; only the bell tower, right, and the office building beneath remain. The clock still keeps time.

The row of houses in the background of this 1912 photograph of Ruthvenfield was provided for employees of Ruthvenfield Bleachworks; their children will have attended the school on the left. Although the bleachworks closed in the 1950s, the scene is surprisingly little changed today: the houses (called Grey Row) are still lived in, the school still serves as Ruthvenfield Primary School, and even the railings in the foreground are still present.

Although Almondbank is located off main roads, it stands at the point where the River Almond leaves its defile to enter more open country for its last few miles down to the River Tay. The river made it a focal point for the district's water-powered textile-finishing industry. There were four important works close by, and the village prospered accordingly. This is an untypically deserted view of Main Street, looking north around 1900. The large building on the right, its prominent quoins contrasting with pale brickwork, was Almondbank's branch of the City of Perth Co-operative Society.

This photograph was taken about halfway up Almondbank Main Street, still looking north. Just out of sight is the bridge over the Almond. Of the two shops on the left, the first was a grocer, the second the village post office. The latter already offered a public telephone; the telephone service became a Post Office monopoly in 1911. Road traffic is conspicuous by its absence, and the road surface is as yet untarred. Marks in its surface appear to be those of carts and carriages.

Almondbank Main Street, looking south in 1909. Even at that date motor traffic had yet to supplant the horse, but the village had a mains water supply, albeit to standpipes such as the one seen here. A gas supply is confirmed by the presence of street lamps.

The rear of the houses lining Main Street, seen from the east bank of the Almond in 1909. The sloping site meant that many of the houses had more storeys at the back than at the front. The weir in the foreground, formerly a mill dam, was used to divert water from the river into the lade which fed Pitcairnfield Bleachworks.

The bowling green at Almondbank, seen here about 1911, lies directly across the river from the viewpoint of the previous picture, between the river bank and Main Street. The Almond Valley Bowling Club, which is now over 120 years old, still flourishes on the same site although the rustic shelter on the far side of the green has since been replaced by a larger pavilion to the left of the green.

A motor charabanc, probably a Milnes-Daimler of about 1907, picks up its passengers in Almondbank Main Street. Most of them appear to be emerging from Scroggie Hill, and since they are in their best clothes one may guess that it is a Sunday school outing or some similar occasion. On the other hand, long and deep shadows cast by a western sun clearly indicate an evening scene: maybe the excursionists have been visiting Almondbank and are now on their way home. There is a bus stop in the same location today.

Almondbank Station was served by trains between Perth and Crieff. It was on the edge of the village, half a mile south of Main Street, so passenger traffic must have been hit hard by the establishment of a bus service. The photograph dates from after 1922, when the London, Midland & Scottish and London & North Eastern Railways – their poster boards can be seen – were formed. From the sidings in the background, beyond the bridge, an unusual private industrial railway ran down to the bleachworks at Huntingtowerfield and Pitcairnfield. It was electrified at 500 volts D.C. with overhead wiring, tramway-style, and was used until 1962. The Perth–Crieff line had been closed to passengers in 1951 and was finally closed to goods traffic in 1967. Almondbank Station building is now a private house.

Tibbermuir Station was sometimes referred to as 'Tibbermuir Siding' or 'Tibbermuir Crossing', but as can be seen here there was a platform and a passenger shelter, and passenger trains called there. It was the next station west of Almondbank on the Perth, Almond Valley & Methven Railway, which opened in 1858. This was later extended to Crieff, and became part of the Caledonian Railway. Mrs Hay, a local lady whose *Reminiscences of Tibbermore and District* was published in 1927, recalled that when the train first went through it was known as 'the Methven Coffee Pot'.

Pedestrian access, direct if somewhat precarious, to Woodend Mill from Braehead and Pitcairngreen was provided by the 'Shoggly Brig' (or 'Shoogly Brig') over the River Almond. Huxley, in *The Almond Valley Past and Present*, mentions discussing it with elderly male residents who all recalled getting it to shoogle to make the girls scream, while being at variance with one another about how it was actually made to do so. The buildings partly hidden by the trees appear more clearly in the next picture: central in the middle distance is Woodend Mill, one of many mills powered by water drawn from the river. This photograph dates from 1909; the bridge itself has long since been swept away.

Woodend, upsteam from Almondbank, in 1909. Concealed below the bushy brow immediately in front of the photographer is the River Almond flowing from right to left beneath the Shoggly Brig. It then turns to flow southwards at the foot of the cliffs in the background. The lade providing water to Woodend Mill, left, can be seen. Formerly a paper mill, and then used for weaving, by 1901 Woodend had become a beetling mill. Beetling – or beating – was an important process in finishing cloth: in a beetle machine, innumerable wooden hammers, arranged beside one another, were raised mechanically to fall successively onto cloth revolving round a roller. According to MacKay in *The Bleachfields of Perth* this closed the cloth up to give it a wavy, watered appearance, much desired, and at the end of the nineteenth century there were 108 beetle machines installed in mills along the River Almond. Beetling was gradually superseded by other processes during the mid-twentieth century and Woodend Mill is long closed.

Moulinalmond House, formerly called Moulin Almond, is located north of Almondbank. The house dates from the 1840s, but had been much extended a few years before this photograph was taken in 1912 (the extension has paler stonework than the original house).

We have now moved to the northeast side of the River Almond, and are looking southwards down Bridgeton Brae towards the bridge which is out of sight round the bend at its foot; Almondbank Main Street lies beyond. St Serf's church, right, had been consecrated four years before this view was photographed in 1909. Originally the Free Church, it still serves the Church of Scotland today.

Bridgeton, Almondbank.

The background to this picture can be seen to be identical to the subject of the last, and is still recognisable today although the foreground is totally altered. The sharp bends in the road were eliminated during the Second World War to facilitate the passage of extra-long vehicles carrying aircraft components to and from Royal Naval Aircraft Stores which were established in the vicinity. Straightening was achieved by continuing the line of the road uphill to the left of this scene, and the land in the foreground of this picture was later used for a private house and its garden. In the picture the nearest house is of a type once locally familiar – designed for occupancy by several families, the outside stair gave direct access to the upper floor for those living there.

Pitcairngreen, formerly 'Pitcairn Green', was founded in the 1780s with the intention that it would provide housing for workers at the extensive cotton mills then recently established at Cromwellpark, on the Almond upstream from Woodend. The *Statistical Account* of the 1790s described it as a village in infancy, although it was predicted that it might one day rival Manchester. Changes in industrial processes, which were absorbed by Manchester, passed Pitcairngreen by however: much of the intended workers' housing was never built and it became and remains a pleasant village laid out around a green. The nearest, most prominent building was the smith's house with smithy adjoining, and to its right can be discerned some of the lime trees which formed the 'queer tree avenue' seen more closely in the next few pictures.

For Edwardian visitors coming by the road from Almondbank, arrival in Pitcairngreen was announced by the appearance, on either side of the road, of two remarkable rows of lime trees, pollarded and trained, or 'pleached', so that their upper branches intertwined. It was known as the 'Queer Tree Avenue' and in winter, bare of leaves, it did indeed justify the name. Part of the avenue survived into the 1950s.

In summer, abundant foliage turned Pitcairngreen's rows of lime trees into a series of green and leafy arches: the manner in which they were trained was hidden, and perhaps mystifying to visitors.

A view of Pitcairngreen, looking along the north side of the green itself, from about 1920. Like Almondbank, Pitcairngreen had a water supply through standpipes such as the one seen here.

Outbreaks of plague and pestilence were all too common during mediaeval times, and the last and possibly worst visitation of 'the pest' came in 1645; it was particularly severe in Perth. Bessie Bell and Mary Gray were the daughters of local lairds, and great friends. They decided to retreat together to a thatched bower at a remote spot near the River Almond, to sit out the plague until it passed – or so we are informed by the once-famous tragic ballad about their story. But the pest caught up with them, in one version of the tale because they were visited by an admirer, who presented them with a pearl necklace he had purchased from someone who had earlier stolen it from a plague victim. Sadly both girls died and the people of Methven, for fear of infection, would not allow their bodies to be brought across the Almond for burial in the kirkyard. The girls were buried together, close to where they died, and a landowner later marked their grave and had it consecrated. Later still, it was enclosed with the railings seen here. The picture dates from around 1903. A century on, grave and railings are still intact, sheltered by the branches of a large yew tree in a secluded place below a steep bank and close to the river, not far from Lynedoch Cottage.

Methven, seen from the north, about 1915. Though not large, and despite its proximity to Perth, Methven has a long history which stretches back to before mediaeval times. The parish church, seen in the middle distance on the left, is comparatively young and dates only from the 1780s; its ornamental spire is an addition of the 1820s. The building to its right, however, with crow-stepped gables, survives from the earlier church of late-mediaeval origin. On the houses, ready availability of slates, from quarries not far away, had meant that thatch had given way early to slate roofs, and Methven people had a reputation for good health and long lives.

Methven Manse was built in the Tudor style about 1831, and is seen here in 1912. It survives today as a private house.

Passing through Methven, the main road from Perth to Crieff had been turnpiked in the 1790s and for many years thereafter was regarded as part of the principal coach road between Dundee, Perth and Glasgow. By Edwardian times that importance had gone: Methven had inherited a main street that was still broad and straight, but empty.

A Morris Cowley makes its way sedately along the main road through Methven in 1925. The road is now part of the A85 trunk road, Perth to Oban, and the amount of traffic upon it would astonish the bystanders in this picture. Back in 1925 however it appears that the Post Office, which then had a monopoly of telegraph and telephone services, had already recognised the importance of the road as a trunk route, or so it appears from the large quantity of cross-arms, with insulators carrying telephone and telegraph wires, to be seen on the poles which line the road.

Station Road, Methven, is much changed since this view of about 1919, although the church spire still stands where it always has. The station itself, shown in the next illustration, has long been closed (to passengers as early as 1937 and goods in 1964) and its site is now used for industry.

Kildrummie Station (Ian Maclaren)

Reids Methven Series.

Methven Station, seen around 1907. When the railway was extended to Crieff, the extension diverged about a mile short of Methven, which was left as the terminus of a short branch line. The postcard from which this view is reproduced has two main points of interest. Firstly, It is captioned 'Kildrummie', the name acquired by Methven in the fiction of Ian Maclaren. Entertaining accounts of travel over the Methven branch, and the characters to be found there, appear in at least two of his most popular books; he called the branch line 'the most remarkable railway in the empire'. Secondly, the locomotive, Caledonian Railway No. 1167, was a rarity as it was one of only four Forney-type 0-4-4 tank locomotives built for use in the UK. The type originated in the USA and even there it was not widely used, although it was successful and popular on the New York elevated railways, and the narrow gauge railroads of Maine.

Methven Public School, which dates from 1910, was still new when this photograph was taken. It is still in use as Methven Primary School, although modern additions now partially conceal this building. The apparent division into boys' and girls' sides has also disappeared.

Standing high on a ridge and looking out over the plain, Methven Castle is the most prominent building in the district – 'prominent', that is, in both its senses of 'conspicuous', and 'distinguished'. There has been a castle of some sort here for many centuries – possibly as long as a millennium – and it played its part in the tangled political history of mediaeval Scotland. The central part of the castle seen in this view of the northern entrance dates from around 1680, when Renaissance features were blending with Scottish tradition; the two extensive wings were additions of about 1800. Those have both disappeared: the western wing before the late 1970s when the future of the castle was in doubt, and the eastern subsequently. However, the central seventeenth-century building has been sympathetically restored.

Keillour Castle is about three miles west of Methven and, rather like Balgowan House (illustrated on the inside front cover), was built around 1877 on the site of an earlier building. Red sandstone was used to build a castle supposedly inspired by those of the Rhineland. The author's late father-in-law, who was a boy at Trinity College, Glenalmond (illustrated in later pictures), between 1918 and 1922, recalled happy days out at Keillour Castle which then belonged to a family called Black. Keillour Castle has fared better than Balgowan House and is still a private residence.

Lawmuir House was, and is, about half a mile to the north of Methven, but the main interest of this picture of *c.*1906 lies with the ponies in the foreground. According to records of the Shetland Pony Stud-Book Society (which was formed in 1890 and is the oldest of the UK native breed societies) Lawmuir House was the residence of G.A. Miller from 1904 until about 1917. There he bred registered pedigree Shetland ponies, using 'Lawmuir' as the stud name. A distinguished member of the society, he became its president in 1910.

The fictional place name 'Drumtochty', used by Ian Maclaren in his books set in the district, became famous enough to be adopted in reality for this large boarding house or similar establishment on the northern outskirts of Methven. It was here, in 1897, that James Wilson was instrumental in forming a Masonic lodge for Methven. Called 'Lodge Kildrummie 906', initially it met in the 'recreation room' of the house.

According to the caption originally printed on it, this picture shows 'Drumtochty School'. In *Beside the Bonnie Briar Bush*, the story which first made Ian Maclaren famous, he describes Drumtochty's 'new school house' on 'an open space beside the main road to Perth, treeless and comfortless, built of red, staring stone with a playground for the boys and another for the girls and a trim, snug-looking teacher's house, all very neat and symmetrical and well regulated…' But the story, set in earlier times, revolves around 'the auld schule-house'. Despite Maclaren's measured disapproval, the school seen in this picture has lasted well, and serves today as Logiealmond Primary School.

For hundreds of years, the focal point of Logiealmond was Logie House. This was the home of the Drummonds of Logiealmond, who were the lairds from the sixteenth century until the nineteenth. Logie House overlooked the River Almond about two miles east of Harrietfield, and this part of it with the tower at the northwest corner probably dated from the sixteenth century. In 1846 the house and estate were sold to the Earl of Mansfield of Scone Palace. By the end of the century, the part of the house seen in this 1904 photograph was derelict.

This elegant mansion was added onto the east side of Logie House in the eighteenth century. By the latter half of the nineteenth century it was being used as a granary but it was then restored, as this photograph of about 1911 shows. The older house was restored also and photographs taken in 1969, now in the collection of the Royal Commission on the Ancient and Historical Monuments of Scotland, show all apparently complete at that date. Nevertheless the entire building was demolished between January and March 1970.

Readers of Ian Maclaren knew Logiealmond Parish Church as 'Drumtochty Kirk'. It was located at Chapelhill; there had been a church there since the 1640s or thereabouts, but by the 1830s it was ruinous. It was then rebuilt into the church shown here but by the mid 1970s this was again a ruin. The walls were pulled down and levelled at shoulder height, and the interior filled in and also levelled.

Drumtochty Village

Despite the caption, the subject of this postcard is in reality Harrietfield, central to Logiealmond district (which Ian Maclaren called 'Drumtochty'). The two most prominent houses, on the left, have gone, but otherwise the scene is little changed today apart from a tarmac surface on the road. The village pub, up a side street, was shown as the 'Drumtochty Tavern' on the 1901 Ordnance Survey map and is still in business today.

RESULT OF GALE
GLENALMOND 28-1-27

The Cairnies estate, northwest of Methven and south of the Almond, was famous for its conifers, so the effect of the great gale of 28 January 1927 was severely felt. The Methven–Buchanty road was closed by fallen trees for a day or more. Nearby in the grounds of Trinity College, Glenalmond, it was estimated that 2,000 trees had been brought down, and the slates were stripped from the roofs of the chapel and the dining hall. Clearing fallen timber must have been laborious in those days. Chainsaws and hard hats alike are conspicuous by their absence in this photograph, and power to move the sawn timber was still provided by a horse.

The Cairnies estate is of some antiquity, and by the nineteenth century was in the hands of the Patton family. The Cairnies House, seen here around 1900, was originally an inn and the owner used Annfield close by. So it was at Annfield in 1842 that the then owner George Patton entertained a young W.E. Gladstone, not yet famous as a politician, and his friend J.R. Hope with grouse and champagne. It seems he entertained them so well that they took the decision there and then to accept Patton's offer (out of several others) of a site on the Cairnies estate for a college which they proposed to found. This college was intended partly to train Episcopalian clergy, and partly to educate 'the children of the gentry and others', and thus was to board and educate up to 200 youths. It took form as Trinity College, Glenalmond. Eventually, in 1946, the Cairnies House itself was bought by the college to become a boarding house.

Trinity College, Glenalmond, was opened in 1847; although the theological side referred to on the previous page was moved to Edinburgh thirty years later, the boys' boarding school developed into a well-known establishment. In recent years it has become co-educational, and altered its name to Glenalmond College. This picture dates from around 1900 and shows the main college buildings from the southwest, with the chapel in the right background. In 1927 a house for the 'warden' or headmaster was added to the right of the main buildings, where the trees are in the picture.

Below: As many as 105 old boys of Glenalmond served in the Boer War and eleven lost their lives. On 20 October 1906 Field Marshal Earl Roberts of Kandahar, VC, who had been the victorious British commander-in-chief during the war, visited the school to open formally the library which had been built as a memorial. Afterwards the Field Marshall inspected the college cadet corps.

FIELD MARSHAL LORD ROBERTS & GENERAL McBEAN
INSPECTING CADET CORPS, TRINITY COLLEGE, GLENALMOND,
ON 20TH OCT. 1906.

Right: The gate lodge for Trinity College, Glenalmond, located where Front Avenue joins the Methven–Buchanty road, was built in 1863/64 for £761.3s.0d. By 1907, the date of this photograph, it contained a post and telegraph office; a telephone had been installed the previous year. In 1928 the wall to the right was demolished and a new entrance to Front Avenue provided without any height restriction; this in turn was closed off within the past few years when another entrance, further along the road, was built. Meanwhile, in 1967 the post office had closed and the lodge became staff accommodation.

The Cairnies Smithy stood on the north side of the Methven–Buchanty road, in the angle where Trinity College's Back Avenue joined it. It was built during the 1860s and was kept busy shoeing the many horses used not only on farms round about, but also to provide transport for people and goods between the college and Methven Station. The building was purchased by the college in 1930, used as a store, and eventually demolished in 1959.

Engineering Dept., College, Glen Almond

Trinity College was a pioneer of small-scale hydro-electricity generation. As early as 1895 the decision was taken to light the college by electricity, and expenditure of £3,500 was authorised for the purpose. Within a bend in the River Almond below the college – the river itself is hidden by trees in this view – stood Halley's Mill, which was both corn mill and sawmill. It was purchased with adjoining land and the generating station, with water turbine, was installed. The station incorporated a maintenance workshop. In 1906 the buildings were extended, additional plant installed, and the Engineering Department, to teach engineering, was established. The buildings containing generating station and teaching department appear in the centre of this picture of 1909, with Harrietfield village in the far distance on the right. The teaching department was moved closer to the college proper in 1926, but the generating station served until the mains arrived in 1949/50.

GLENTULCHAN,
GLENALMOND.

Glentulchan, sometimes known as 'Glentulcan' and since the mid-twentieth century as Tulchan House, stands beside the River Almond (which flows between it and the trees in the background) a couple of miles upstream from Glenalmond College. As long ago as the 1680s the lands of Tulchan were joined with the neighbouring estate of Gorthie, which itself had a history going back into the middle ages. In 1815 Gorthie was bought by George Mercer, of a noted Perth family, who had profited as a merchant in Calcutta. According to the *New Statistical Account* of 1837, Mercer of Gorthie was not among the resident landowners in the parish, but had a 'neat cottage' in a 'small but sweet spot' beside the Almond east of Buchanty. This sounds like the origin of Glentulchan, and by the 1870s at the latest the Mercers appear to have been resident there, for they established a family burial ground nearby. Nevertheless the house changed hands in 1904, and has done so on several occasions subsequently – although descendants of successive owners recall it with affection. It was enlarged several times, most recently at a date between 1910 and the mid 1920s, the period from which this photograph is believe to date. The appearance of Tulchan House has not altered since, and it remains a private house.

Glenalmond House, north of the River Almond, dates from the early 1830s at which time the Glenalmond Estate, like The Cairnies, belonged to the Pattons. It was rebuilt after a fire in 1907, just before this picture was taken about 1909. By that date the owner was Sir Arthur Henderson, later Lord Farringdon. Henderson was a City financier and chairman of the Great Central Railway Company which had built the last of the great Victorian main-line railways, reaching London Marylebone from the North of England in 1899. Regrettably it never prospered and much of it was closed during the 1960s. Glenalmond House has fared better and underwent substantial renovations and improvements to be made around the year 2000 and subsequently.

The larger of the two houses, in the background of this picture of Buchanty, was marked as a school on the 1901 Ordnance Survey map. The road from Methven passes in front of them. Both houses survive although the school is now a private dwelling.